ROADS

BY CASS R. SANDAK

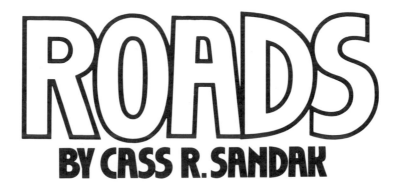

An Easy-Read Modern Wonders Book

Franklin Watts
New York/London/Toronto/Sydney
1984

Over: a line-marking machine divides a newly
laid section of highway into lanes.

For my mother and the roads
we have traveled together

R.L. 3.8 Spache Revised Formula

Cover photograph courtesy of Commonwealth of Pennsylvania

Photographs courtesy of: *Shostal Associates:* pp. 1, 6 (bottom right), 7 (bottom right), 8
(top left), 11 (bottom), 20 (left), 23 (top right), 25 (bottom); Frank Sloan: pp. 4, 6 (left), 11
(top), 18 (bottom left and right), 27 (bottom); the author: pp. 7 (left), 8 (right), 14, 21 (top
right), 23 (top left and bottom right and left), 24; *Ewing Galloway:* pp. 9, 19 (bottom
right), 20 (right), 21 (top left); American Airlines: p. 12; *Bettmann Archive:* pp. 13 (left
and right), 15, 17 (bottom), 18 (top); *Culver Pictures:* p. 17 (top); American Trucking
Association: p. 19 (bottom left); Caterpillar Tractor Company: p. 21 (bottom); American
Road and Transportation Builders Association: p. 25 (top); Commonwealth of
Pennsylvania: p. 27 (top); Andrews & Clark: p. 28 (top); Florida Department of
Transportation: p. 29 (top); Alaska Department of Tourism: p. 29 (bottom).

Diagrams by Jane Kendall

Library of Congress Cataloging in Publication Data

Sandak, Cass R.
  Roads.

  (Easy-read modern wonders book)
  Includes index.
  Summary: Discusses the nature and history of
roads built in ancient and modern times for travel
by wheeled vehicles.
  1. Roads—Juvenile Literature. [1. Roads] I. Title.
II. Series.
TE149.S26 1984   625.7   83-25993
ISBN 0-531-04710-5

Contents

Large roads called freeways connect many parts
of southern California with downtown Los Angeles.

What Is a Road?

A **road** is a path or strip of land that lets people, animals, and goods travel from place to place easily. Roads may be paved or unpaved, but they should have a surface that is made for travel by wheeled vehicles.

Roads are used by cars, buses, and trucks as well as by people on foot. They speed the movement of people, freight, and information from one place to another.

Roads make it easy to get to cities or to the countryside. Some roads lead down into deep canyons or up to high mountain tops. Thanks to bridges, roads can span great bodies of water or cross through marshlands. Tunnels let roads pass right through the centers of mountains. Sometimes instead of a tunnel, a notch is cut right through a mountain, open to the sky. This is called a **cut**.

Roads are used for business and travel. They are needed to ship raw materials and finished goods from one place to another. They are also used to carry produce from farms to markets. Roads helped early market towns grow into great cities.

Roads can unite the people of one country. They can also bring together the people of different nations. Canada, Mexico, and the United States are linked to Central America and South America by a road system called the Pan American Highway. This road makes it possible to drive from the northernmost parts of Canada or Alaska all the way down to the tip of South America. This is a distance of more than 10,000 miles (16,000 km). International road and highway systems link the countries of Europe together.

Good roads reduce the time we need to spend traveling. They give us more time to do other things. They make travel, visiting, and vacationing easier.

Different Kinds of Roads

Left: an unpaved country road. *Right:* a section of the Trans-Canada Highway.

Road is a general term. There are many words that mean special types of roads. A lane is a narrow

country road. A **street** is usually a road that passes through a city or town and has buildings along it. An **avenue** is a wide road or street. A wide road or street lined with trees may be called a **boulevard**. A **parkway** is usually a scenic, tree-lined road or **highway** reserved for passenger cars.

Today any main road may be called a highway, but the first highways were just that. These roads were raised above the ground and had ditches on both sides for better drainage. This made it easier for horses and carriages to travel over them.

Throughways, turnpikes, freeways, and expressways are all different names for **superhighways**. These roads have many lanes and are safer for high-speed driving. They are called **limited access roads**. Cars or trucks can enter or leave the traffic only at certain points. Some of them are **toll roads** that require drivers to pay a fee to use them.

Left: a street scene on the island of Crete.
Right: part of the Autobahn near Hamburg, Germany.

Left: the Ringstrasse in Vienna, Austria. The wide boulevard circles the oldest part of the city. *Right:* Naples, Italy. The narrow, crowded street is typical of the old sections of many European cities.

What Roads Tell Us

Roads often tell us a lot about the history of cities and towns. In England, old Roman settlements are usually indicated by the crossing of two main streets. In some cities, broad boulevards mark the area where ancient city walls once stood. There are boulevards in some American cities that follow the routes where old canals were filled in.

The oldest sections of many modern cities, including London, New York, and Boston have some streets that seem to wind around without any plan. Streets like these were once paths that wound their way through farms and fields long before the cities grew up around them.

Paris, France, and Washington, D.C., have some streets that radiate out from a central point, like the spokes of a wheel, in a "hub" pattern.

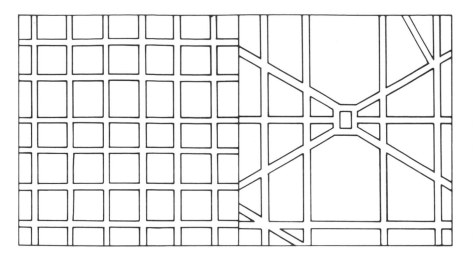

Two kinds of street patterns. *Left:* a rectangular "grid" plan. *Right:* a radial or "hub" plan.

Philadelphia, New York, and other cities have a rectangular "grid" layout. Both of these patterns are the result of careful city planning.

In the midwestern United States, roads that cross acre after acre of flat farmland sometimes jog unexpectedly to the right or left. These roads often indicate the boundaries between lands granted to different farmers when the areas were settled in the 1800s.

Broadway, in New York City, is one of the most famous streets in the world. It follows an old Indian path that ran north to south on Manhattan Island. It may even have started out as an animal trail!

9

Parts of a Road

A road surface may be **unpaved** or **paved**. An unpaved road usually has a dirt or gravel surface. Paved means that the road has been prepared with a hard surface made of special materials laid over a **base** and **subgrade**. Painted lines divide the **pavement** into **lanes**. A **lane** is a single line of traffic.

Roads are often built so that they are slightly higher in the middle. The higher part is called the **crown**. It helps rainwater to run off.

Curves in a road may be **banked**, or have a slightly tilted surface. Sometimes this banking is called **superelevation**. Banking helps cars stay on the road during turns, especially at high speeds.

The area along the side of a paved road is called the **shoulder**, or **verge**. Often it has a surface of gravel. It is not used for driving but for stopping and for making repairs. The shoulder also allows rainwater to run off from the main road surface.

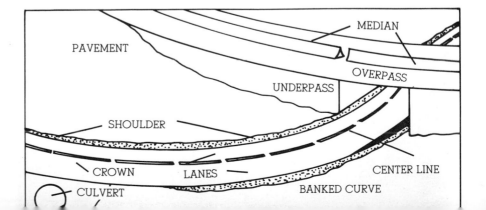

Road planners make sure that roads have good sightlines. Drivers need to see at least 600 feet (183 m) ahead.

On modern superhighways, lanes of traffic that go in opposite directions are separated by a strip of ground called the **median**. These roads are called **divided highways**.

A **grade level crossing** is where roads cross each other at the same level. Because they are dangerous, they are often the scenes of accidents. Many modern roads are designed and built to avoid these dangers. **Overpasses** are usually bridges that carry traffic over a crossroad. And **underpasses** take traffic under a crossroad.

A traffic **loop** is a curving road that makes it easier to get on or off a highway without crossing lanes of traffic. These roads curve over or under lanes of fast-moving traffic.

A cloverleaf has four big loops that look like a four-leaf clover from the air.

11

The Story of Roads

The Beginnings

The story of roads begins with the tracks and trails of animals and early people. Many of these were paths to a salt lick or water hole. Or they might have led from a cave to a hunting ground or vegetable patch.

Paths are not always the shortest way between two points. But they are usually the fastest and easiest, avoiding trees and rocks. Little by little people learned to improve the paths by moving rocks or cutting down trees. These were the first roads.

When people learned to farm, they began to live in settled communities. In this way roads linking houses and villages developed. Trade grew and became important on these primitive roads, which were traveled on foot and by beasts

Even today this trail in the Grand Canyon is used by people on pack animals.

of burden. After the wheel was invented, chariots, carts, and wagons called for smoother and better roads.

One of the oldest roads is the Royal Road of Persia. It was built between 1400 and 500 BC. It was about 1,600 miles (2,575 km) long and connected the provinces with the capital city of Susa. It was used as a route for relay teams of messengers who together covered 100 miles (160 km) a day.

The rise of cities and empires led to the development of improved roads. Early roads made communication and military campaigns easier. Roads allowed the movement of supplies and aided the collection of taxes and tributes.

Roman Roads

The Romans were the first ancient people to build roads on a large scale. Their roads were designed to last and were so solidly constructed that parts of them are still in use today.

Left: a street in ancient Pompeii. Large stepping stones allowed people to cross from one side of the street to the other. Chariot wheels passed between the stones.
Right: the Appian Way was built between 312 and 244 B.C. and is still in use.

Layers of a Roman road.

A) large, flat stones
B) small stones and gravel in mortar
C) rocks set in mortar
D) large, flat stones in mortar

A

B

C

D

The Romans built more than 53,000 miles (84,800 km) of paved roads. They crisscrossed many parts of the Roman Empire.

The Roman road builders first made a base for the road out of stone blocks. Next came a layer of small stones tightly packed together and bound with cement. On top of that was another layer of pebbles and rubble set in cement. The surface was made up of large slabs of hard stone closely fitted together. Roman roads were from 3 to 6 feet (.9 to 1.8 m) thick.

Roman roads were generally straight even where the land was uneven. Roman engineers cut across hills, through swamps and forests, and over streams. Only mountains forced builders to swerve from a straight course.

Roads of the Ancient Americas

For the most part, Indian trails were rough footpaths. The North American Indians and the Indians of eastern South America usually traveled by water on streams and rivers. But the Incas, the Indians of South America's Andes Mountains, built a fine road system a thousand years ago. Some of the Inca roads wind through mountain passes so steep that they are built in steps. Runners and llamas used these roads, but wheeled vehicles did not.

The Inca highways on the coastal plain were connected to higher plateaus by roads more than 2,000 miles (3,216 km) long and 20 feet (6 m) wide. They were made of stones and a very hard mortar. In most places, Inca roads were built on top of high embankments of earth.

European Roads After the Romans

Caravans and trade routes first brought the West into contact with the East and its lively market for silks and spices. In the Middle Ages, some roads developed out of routes that pilgrims traveled on their way to shrines of the saints all over Europe.

The Crusaders followed many well-known paths in their journeys across Europe to the Holy Land.

Until the 1700s and 1800s, most roads in Europe were the remains of early Roman roads. Or else they were deeply rutted dirt roads that made travel slow and uncomfortable. Horses and sedan chairs were the usual forms of transportation for people. Even coaches were rare. Pack animals transported goods over land.

A New Era Begins

Around 1800, Thomas Telford and John McAdam, two British engineers, developed improved ways to pave roads. They used layers of gravel and crushed stone moistened with water and packed down to make a pavement about 10 inches (25 cm) thick. Macadam pavements were later bound together with tar. The pavement was also raised in the middle for water runoff. The **crown macadam road**, or **macadamized** surface, is still a feature of rural areas in the United States and Great Britain.

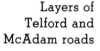

Layers of Telford and McAdam roads

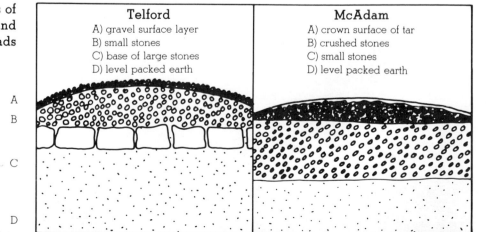

Telford	McAdam
A) gravel surface layer	A) crown surface of tar
B) small stones	B) crushed stones
C) base of large stones	C) small stones
D) level packed earth	D) level packed earth

The Boston Post Road, between New York City and Boston, Massachusetts, was one of the best roads in colonial America.

Roads in the Early United States

Roads played an important part in the growth of the United States. In many places, settlers broadened old Indian footpaths into roads and wagon trails.

In the 1800s the National Road helped settlers who wanted to move into the Ohio Valley or go even farther west. It stretched from Maryland to Illinois. And the Oregon Trail allowed settlers, traders, and trappers an easier route from Missouri all the way to Oregon.

Daniel Boone and the Wilderness Road helped open up the land beyond the coastal areas of the original thirteen colonies.

17

The Santa Fe Trail opened up the Southwest with a route from western Missouri to New Mexico.

In some parts of the country private companies built special toll roads that they operated for profit. These roads, called **turnpikes**, opened up routes to new places. They were named turnpikes after a type of tollgate that blocked the entrance to the road. A gatekeeper opened the road for passage, for a small fee, or toll. Some settlers, who refused to pay the fees, often made their own "shun pikes" around the toll booths.

In the mid-1800s railroads and canals were the main means of travel. Roadbuilding only became an important branch of engineering around 1900. Users of the newly invented automobiles and bicycles needed better roads on which to travel.

Where timber was plentiful, roads were paved with wood. Whole logs were laid down (left) to form bumpy corduroy roads. In other places, pieces of flat timber were made into plank roads (right).

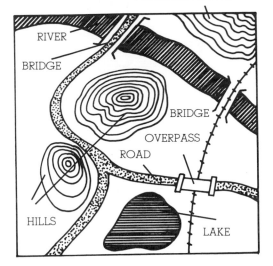

Layout of road plan on a contour map

MOUNTAIN SLOPE
RIVER
BRIDGE
BRIDGE
OVERPASS
ROAD
HILLS
LAKE

Road Building

Planning

Building a road takes years of planning. In the early stages, the ground is studied and surveyed. Soil samples are analyzed. Road designers decide whether to go over, around, under or through natural obstacles like hills or swamps.

Traffic engineers need to know many things. Who will use the road? Will the road be used for long-distance, high-speed driving? Engineers must plan for the future number and types of vehicles. They must decide whether bridges and tunnels are needed. They need to know the

Left: the roadwork begins. *Right:* roads through mountainous areas must be designed with sharp curves called switchbacks.

number of lanes, the sharpness of the curves, and how much the highway may have to be banked.

Road lighting and drainage must be planned early. Water from rain, streams, or melted snow could wash away the roadbed. **Culverts** help prevent this. A culvert is a large pipe that is installed under the road where it passes over a ditch or stream.

After the route has been planned on a map, stakes with marking flags on them are set in the ground to show where the road will be built. Road builders use these flags as a guide.

Preparation of the Roadbed

Left: explosives are used to blast rock. *Right:* bulldozers prepare the roadbed alongside a river valley.

First the site is cleared. Bulldozers knock down trees and pull up roots. Rocks are pushed out of the way or blasted with dynamite. Buildings may need to be torn down or moved.

Many kinds of earth-moving equipment are used to clear the roadbed. **Backhoes** have scoops for digging and for moving piles of dirt. **Rippers** can cut through layers of rock, breaking them into smaller pieces. **Crawlers** are pieces of machinery that have great belt treads instead of wheels. Even where the ground is not solid, these treads give traction for digging up dirt and rock. **A front end loader** is like a big shovel that carries dirt into trucks to be hauled away.

A steam shovel (left) and a backhoe (right) are both used to scoop out the roadbed.

Scrapers and **graders** make a smooth, straight path. Scrapers help to prepare a flat, even surface that will become the roadbed. Some areas are filled in and others are scraped away. Crooked paths are straightened, high places are leveled out, and holes are filled in.

Graders are used to smooth and level the road surface. Graders also shape the shoulders alongside the roadbed.

21

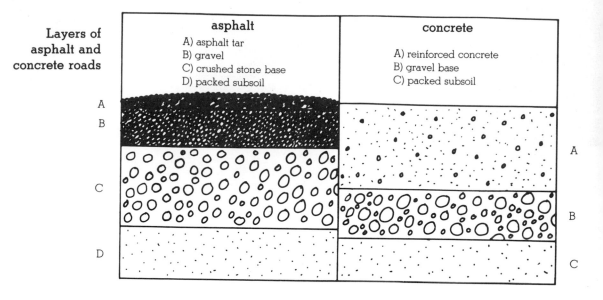

Layers of
asphalt and
concrete roads

asphalt
A) asphalt tar
B) gravel
C) crushed stone base
D) packed subsoil

concrete
A) reinforced concrete
B) gravel base
C) packed subsoil

Building the Road

After the roadbed has been cleared and smoothed, construction of the actual road begins. Highway work usually takes place in sections, with teams of road builders working on each section.

First a layer of gravel is laid over the firmly packed-down subsoil. This gravel layer is called the **subbase.** It may be from 4 inches (10 cm) to as much as a foot (.3 m) thick. The gravel is packed down with rollers.

Next comes a layer of crushed stone. This will be the **road base.** Heavy rollers pack down the gravel and stone into the earth. **A sheepsfoot roller** is used. This is a roller that has small steel spikes shaped like sheeps' hooves in it.

Paving

Paving is usually done with **concrete** or **asphalt**. Surfacing proceeds in stages. Asphalt is a thick, tarlike substance made from petroleum mixed with small stones. The asphalt is laid over an extra layer of crushed stone. It is poured down hot and then is leveled by hand and smoothed with heavy rollers.

Concrete is a mixture of cement, sand, and gravel that is combined with water. It is laid right over the base layer. Concrete is poured into steel forms that hold the liquid concrete in place until it is set. The concrete mixer lays pavement in long sections at one time. As soon as the spreader has leveled the concrete, wire reinforcement is put down. Then more concrete is poured over the reinforcement and it is leveled.

Left: liquid concrete will be poured into steel forms like these. *Right:* a crane with a telescope boom pours concrete into the forms.

Left: workers level a mixture of asphalt and gravel. *Right:* rollers smooth the asphalt surface.

Concrete is "cured," or allowed to set slowly. The covering is kept moist until the concrete has hardened properly without cracking.

A finishing machine smooths the concrete and shapes it to the proper grade. A long mechanical float forces out pockets of air or water from the concrete.

If the road surface were completely smooth it would be very slippery. It must have some roughness or texture. This roughness means that tires can grip the road for better **traction**. To make a textured surface, burlap or stiff brooms are dragged across the concrete while it is still wet. The surface may be "belted," or struck with a canvas strip to produce a swirled, rough finish that will help prevent skids.

In the final step, joints are sawed into the concrete. Diamond-tipped power saws cut the concrete into blocks 60 to 70 feet (18 to 21 m) long. The spaces between these blocks allow the pavement to expand and contract.

A spreading and finishing machine smooths the concrete surface.

Finishing the Road

Once the road has been laid, it is ready for the final details. A special line-marking machine paints the center line and marks the traffic lanes to guide motorists. These lines show where motorists can pass, or overtake, other cars. Later, traffic signals, street lights, guard rails, road signs, and route markers can be put in place.

Roads give jobs to many people. Workers build them. And even after the roads are finished, they must be taken care of. From time to time, roads have to be resurfaced. Toll takers are on duty around the clock on many roads. And in the winter, in many places, snow removal is a big part of road maintenance.

Roads need constant attention. Here a roller resurfaces a road. This kind of maintenance is a year-round job.

Road Signs and Route Markers

NO
STOPPING

YIELD

DO NOT
ENTER

TRAFFIC
SIGNAL AHEAD

SLIPPERY

ROAD
NARROWS

SPEED
LIMIT

NO "U"
TURN

DEER
CROSSING

NO
PEDESTRIANS

Examples of
international
road signs

Road signs warn drivers of intersecting traffic, railroad crossings, falling rocks, and dangerous grades and curves.

Sometimes road signs tell us about kinds of animals we might see. In the West there are frequent signs: CATTLE CROSSING. In the Northeast there are often signs: DEER CROSSING. These signs mark paths that in many cases were established by these animals long before any roads were built through the areas.

Road systems are given route numbers. These numbers help to guide motorists. Drivers can find the way to the places they are going by following the road and route signs and by using road maps.

In North America, roads that run in a general north-to-south direction have odd route numbers. Roads that go between east and west have even numbers. Usually, numbering is lower in the East and North. The higher route numbers are in the West and South. Numbering for interstate routes is somewhat different. An Interstate highway system connects the most important roads in the United States.

Modern highways are clearly marked with large, readable direction signs.

Most developed countries today have highway systems that make travel between cities fast and easy. Germany has its modern **Autobahn** system. And in Italy the **autostrada** links major cities.

The custom of driving on the right developed in the United States, where certain types of horse-drawn wagons had a place for the driver to sit or stand on the left side. In order to see the road, and other drivers, it was necessary to keep the wagon to the right side of the road.

Soon all traffic in the United States kept to the right. When automobiles were invented, they were designed with steering wheels on the left. Because many cars were built this way, most countries adopted the American custom.

A street in modern London, England. Today traffic in all the major countries of the world, except Great Britain, keeps to the right.

Three layers of road and a park on top are supported like shelves on brackets. This is known as cantilevering.

Roads for Tomorrow

In the future, larger highways of ten to twelve lanes will be built. There will be many more vehicles, although they may be of different types. Cars, trucks, and buses may be locked into computerized systems that control speed and traffic flow by radar or other electronic methods.

Soon roads may have high curved edges like racing tracks. These will force cars back on the road if they speed out of control. The road surfaces themselves may have lights set in them to help drivers at night.

At some point in the future, roads themselves may move. Vehicles will be carried along between interchange points, where they can get on or off conveyor devices. Moving pavements for pedestrians are already in use in some airports and shopping malls.

New transport systems may mean that fewer roads will be needed. Air-cushion vehicles that hover above the ground may not need roads at all! Pipeline and tube systems may carry many products, including fuel and raw materials, across the continent. But, for the foreseeable future, roads and the people and vehicles on them will continue to make our modern way of life possible.

Modern roads extend over long stretches of water (top) and through dangerous mountain passes (bottom).

Words About Roads

Asphalt. A thick substance like tar, which is laid over crushed stone to make a hard road surface.

Backhoe. A machine used in road construction. It has a big scoop that digs and moves dirt.

Banking. The tilt of a road surface, usually on a curve. Also called superelevation.

Base. The part of a paved road just under the hard surface.

Cloverleaf. A series of road loops that allow cars to get on or off a large road without crossing lanes of traffic.

Concrete. Cement, sand, and gravel mixed with water. Concrete sets to form a hard, stonelike material.

Corduroy road. An early U.S. road in which whole logs were laid side by side.

Crawler. A machine that digs up rock and dirt. Instead of wheels, it has great belt treads.

Crown. The higher part of the middle of a road. It is usually raised slightly to help drainage.

Culvert. A large pipe installed under a road to take excess water away from the road.

Cut. A notch cut through a large rock or mountain. It is usually open at the top.

Divided highway. A highway with separate lanes of traffic, usually divided by a strip of ground, or median.

Front end loader. A big shovel that takes dirt away from a roadbed during construction.

Grade level crossing. A place where roads cross each other at the same level.

Grader. A road-building machine that smooths and levels a road. It also shapes the shoulder alongside the road.

Highway. A large, main road. The first highways were raised high above the ground, but today many are not.

Lane. A narrow country road. A lane is also a part of a road for a single line of cars.

Limited access road. A road that cars can enter or leave only at certain points.

Loop. A curved road to let cars on or off without crossing lanes of traffic.

Macadamized surface. A road surface of gravel and crushed stone held together by water and tar.

Median. A strip of ground that divides the lanes of traffic on a modern highway.

Overpass. A bridgelike part of a road that carries traffic over a crossroad.

Paved road. A road that has a hard surface.

Pavement. A section of paved road or street.

Plank road. A kind of early U.S. road made from pieces of flat timber laid side by side.

Ripper. A machine that cuts through layers of rock.

Road base. A layer of crushed stone just over the subbase.

Roadbed. The layer of subsoil on which a road is built.

Scraper. A road-building machine that scrapes away the ground to make a flat, smooth roadbed.

Sheepsfoot roller. A roller with spikes shaped like a sheep's hoof. It packs down layers of gravel and stone.

Shoulder. The area along the side of a paved road.

Subbase. The gravel layer of a road just above the subsoil.

Subgrade. The road layer between the roadbed and the surface.

Superelevation. The angle at which a road is tilted on a curve. Also known as banking.

Superhighway. Large, modern road with several lanes of traffic going in each direction. Also called throughway, turnpike, freeway, and expressway.

Turnpike. An early toll road called after a tollgate that blocked the entrance. Often now used as a name for a major modern highway.

Underpass. A short passage under a crossroad.

Unpaved road. A road with a dirt or gravel surface.

Index

G.3t

Roads

Engineering

1984